Ex Libris

Artists in Their Time

Henry Moore

Sally O'Reilly

Franklin Watts
A Division of Scholastic Inc.
New York Toronto London Auckland Sydney
Mexico City New Delhi Hong Kong
Danbury, Connecticut

First published in 2003 by
Franklin Watts
96 Leonard Street
London EC2A 4XD

First American edition published
in 2003 by Franklin Watts
A Division of Scholastic Inc.
90 Sherman Turnpike
Danbury, CT 06816

Series Editor: Adrian Cole
Editor: Susie Brooks
Series Designer: Mo Choy
Art Director: Jonathan Hair
Picture Researcher: Sue Mennell

A CIP catalog record for this title
is available from the Library of Congress.

ISBN 0-531-12241-7 (Lib. Bdg.)
ISBN 0-531-16643-0 (Pbk.)

Printed in Hong Kong, China

Acknowledgements

The following biographical images and the work(s) illustrated have been reproduced by kind permission of The Henry Moore Foundation: The Henry Moore Foundation Archive: 7t, 8, 9t (LH 6), 10t, 11 (LH 43), 17 (LH 59), 18tr, 19t, 27, 30b (LH 339), 32bl (CGM 114), 33, 35 (LH 573), 36b (HMF 3361), 39 (HMF 80 (60)); Courtauld Institute of Art: 20b; Darren Chung: front cover centre (LH 205), front cover br, 23 (LH 205), 26t; Felix H. Mann: 26t; Michel Muller: 6 (HMF 488), 21 (HMF 1077), 43 (HMF 123), 24b, 37 (LH 627); Fox Photos: 28b; Errol Jackson 26b (LH293), 29 (LH 350), 32t, 32br, 38t; Luke Finn: 13 (LH 58), 31 (LH 344); John Hedgecoe: 34t.Arcaid/Alex Bartel: 41t © ADAGP, Paris and DACS, London 2003. Bridgeman Art Library/ Lauros/Giraudon: 30t. Castello Sforzesco, Milan/ Scala Florence: 12b. Didrichsen Art Museum, Helsinki, Finland/Matti Ruotsalainen: 33 © Henry Moore Foundation. Ford Motor Company Limited:41b. Geoscience Features Picture Library/RIDA: 12t. ©Jarrold Publishing/Peter Smith/ with kind permission of the Administrator of Westminster Cathedral: 15b © the Estate of Eric Gill/ Bridgeman Art Library. Leslie Garland Picture Library: 7b/Paul Ridsdale,40/ Leslie Garland. London Transport Headquarters, 55, Broadway, London/Bridgeman Art Library: 14 Tate, London 2003, © The Estate of Jacob Epstein. Courtesy of the Mayor Gallery, London: 18b. Museo Nacional de Antropologia, Mexico City, Mexico/ Bridgeman Art Library:16t. © Board of Trustees, National Gallery of Art, Washington D.C: 36t/Gift of the Morris and Gwendolyn Cafritz Foundation. National Gallery, London/Bridgeman Art Library: 16b. Philadelphia Museum of Art, Pennsylvania, PA/Bridgeman Art Library:38b. Popperfoto: front cover bl, 20t, front cover bc and 24t/Saidman, 25, 28t. Rudolph Staechelin Family Foundation, Basel, Switzerland/Bridgeman Art Library: 9b. Science and Society Picture Library: 22b. ©Tate, London 2003: 10br © Henry Moore Foundation,19b © Alan Bowness, Hepworth Estate,22 The Works of Naum Gabo © Nina Williams,24b © Henry Moore Foundation,27 © Henry Moore Foundation,34b © Bruce McLean. Tate Gallery Archive: 15t. Werner Forman Archive/British Museum 10b.

With special thanks to Emma Stower of The Henry Moore Foundation

Whilst every attempt has been made to clear copyright
should there be any inadvertent omission please apply
in the first instance to the publisher regarding rectification.

Contents

Who Was Henry Moore?

Henry Moore was one of the most important sculptors of modern time. He changed the way people see art by placing huge sculptures outside in cities or the countryside. His work was criticized at first but Moore steadily grew more successful over time. Today, hundreds of Moore's sculptures are on display in parks, city plazas, and major buildings throughout the world.

A VICTORIAN FAMILY

Moore was born in Castleford, Yorkshire, England, in 1898. He was the seventh in a family of eight brothers and sisters. Moore's parents, Raymond and Mary, were a strong influence on the children. Raymond was a coal miner who had great ambitions for his children. By the time Henry was born one brother and two sisters had become teachers. Henry was expected to do the same.

> *"First become qualified as a teacher like your brothers and sisters have done and then change to art if you wish. Be sure that you have some living in your hand."*
>
> Raymond Moore

◄ **The Artist's Mother, 1927, Henry Moore.**
Mary Moore was a loving mother who worked hard looking after her family at home. She suffered from rheumatism in her back and would ask Moore to massage it. He said that this gave him an early understanding of the gentle curves of the human body.

TIMELINE ▶

July 30, 1898	1909	1911	1914	1915	1916	1917	1918
Henry Spencer Moore is born in Castleford, England.	Henry learns about Michelangelo and becomes interested in sculpture.	Moore starts pottery classes with art teacher Alice Gostick.	World War I begins.	Moore becomes a student teacher.	Moore teaches in Castleford.	Moore joins the army. Poisoned by gas in France, he returns to England.	Moore becomes an army physical instructor and returns to France just as the war ends.

▶ Private Moore (front row, far right) with his Civil Service Rifles platoon, 1917.

SCHOOL DAYS

Moore attended his local primary school then won a scholarship to secondary school. He also went to Sunday school, where he discovered the work of Michelangelo (1475-1564) and became interested in sculpture. Moore was good at art and was determined to make it his career. At the age of 17, under his father's firm guidance, he began teaching at his old primary school. However, this did not last long. Moore's teaching career was soon interrupted by World War I.

THE YOUNG SOLDIER

At age 19, Moore was drafted into the British army and sent to fight. He wrote to his old art teacher, Alice Gostick, about the terrible conditions – the noise, the lack of sleep, and how he made drawings of people picking lice from their clothes. During the battle of Cambrai in France, Moore was poisoned by mustard gas and taken back to a hospital in England. When he recovered he spent the rest of the war as a physical training instructor before returning home to Yorkshire, England, in 1919.

THE YORKSHIRE LANDSCAPE

The Yorkshire landscape had a strong effect on Moore. It was a land of contrasts. The countryside has rolling hills and large, open skies, while the local mining industry dotted the area with ugly slag heaps. Moore would always remember the shapes of rocky crags, the mountains of coal, and the smooth pebbles of the Castleford streets. They were to appear in his sculptures throughout his life. As he recalled, "Some things are little on the outside, and rough and common, but I remember the time when the dust and stones of the streets were as precious as gold to my infant eyes."

▲ Rocky outcrops in the Yorkshire Dales.

Becoming a Sculptor

▲ Moore began pottery classes with Alice Gostick while he was still at school. He continued them after the war. This photo, taken in 1919, shows Alice on the far right with Moore on the floor beside her. He said that the lessons "kept him sane" when he was a teacher.

Moore's art teacher, Alice Gostick, remained an important inspiration to him after the war. When he returned from the army, she encouraged him to pursue his art career and found out about grants for people whose education had been interrupted by the war.

A CHANCE TO LEARN

With the help of a grant, Moore enrolled at Leeds School of Art in England. He still lived in Castleford where he attended evening pottery classes so he had to catch a train to Leeds each day.

After a year of studying drawing at the art school, he announced that he wanted to be a sculptor. Moore was very insistent so the school set up a sculpture department with him as its only student for the first year. One of the first people to follow Moore into the department was Barbara Hepworth (1903-75). She became his friend and also a famous artist.

TIMELINE ▶

1919	September 1919	1921
Moore returns to Castleford and takes pottery lessons with Alice Gostick.	Moore enrolls at Leeds School of Art. A sculpture department is set up with Moore as the only student. Moore encounters modern art for the first time on a visit to Sir Michael Sadler's collection.	Moore meets fellow student Barbara Hepworth. He wins a scholarship to the Royal College of Art in London.

HEADING FOR LONDON

Leeds was just the first step for Moore. In 1921, he won a scholarship to study sculpture at the Royal College of Art in London, England. It was during these first years at the college that Moore started to rebel against authority. Most art school training was based on classical and Renaissance art, but Moore wanted to break away from tradition. His teachers insisted that he use pointing machines to copy classical sculpture. Moore refused. Instead, he carved directly into stone with a hammer and chisel. "When I was a student," he later said, "direct carving as an occupation, and as a sculptor's natural way of producing things, was simply unheard of."

◀ *Head of the Virgin*, **1922-23, Henry Moore.** This marble piece is a copy of a classical sculpture, but Moore has made it his own by including part of the original block of stone in the composition. It shows both his skill at lifelike carving and his originality in breaking away from tradition.

GLIMPSES OF MODERNISM

In Victorian times right up to the turn of the 20th century, art in England was mostly academic – it followed traditional teachings from past masters and had a formal style. Moore had been frustrated by the lack of modern art around him until he met Professor Michael Sadler, the Vice-Chancellor of Leeds University. Sadler had a collection that included paintings by Paul Cézanne (1839-1906), Paul Gauguin (1848-1903), Henri Matisse (1869-1954), and Vincent van Gogh (1853-90). It was Gauguin's work more than anyone else's that opened Moore's eyes to the world beyond Victorian art. In 1891, Gauguin had emigrated to Tahiti in order to make island life the focus of his art.

▶ *When Are You Getting Married?*, **1892, Paul Gauguin.** Gauguin was one of the first painters to use color simply as decoration or to create emotion.

Ancient Impact

THE BRITISH MUSEUM

Until the British Museum opened in 1759, Britain did not have a large museum or library. The collection housed in the British Museum originally belonged to Professor Hans Sloane (1660-1753) and consisted of 120,000 specimens, artifacts, prints, drawings, coins, and manuscripts. When Sloane died he left the collection as a gift to the British nation. It was kept in Montagu House but the building was too small for the growing public interest. In 1823, a new home was designed for the collection. This museum was Britain's largest public building and took 30 years to complete.

Today, many items have been transferred to other museums and galleries so the British Museum can focus on ancient cultural objects from around the world.

▲ This bronze Benin plaque from early 17th-century Africa is one of many primitive artifacts on display at the British Museum.

◀ This African mask is like many works that Moore saw in the British Museum. The influence of this kind of primitive art on Moore is clear in his stone *Mask*, 1928 (below right).

In 1921, while studying at the Royal College of Art, Moore discovered Roger Fry's book *Vision and Design* in a library. Reading Fry's essays on ancient art led him to a new fascination – primitive sculpture. From this moment on, Moore spent days in the British Museum drawing ancient sculptures from Egypt, Africa, and Mexico.

ABSTRACT FORMS

The term "primitive" can be used to describe art from many different cultures but does not include European or Oriental art. Whereas European painting and sculpture tends to be lifelike, primitive figures often have dots for eyes and chunky, tubular limbs. In modern art this use of exaggerated and simplified forms is called abstraction. Moore recognized that abstraction can be very expressive and began to style his work in this way.

TIMELINE ▶

1921	1922	1922-23
Moore discovers Roger Fry's book *Vision and Design* and starts regular visits to the British Museum.	Moore begins carving in stone and wood. He carves his first sculpture of a mother and child. His father dies.	Moore discovers a book on contemporary artist Henri Gaudier-Brzeska (1891-1915). This has a strong influence on his work.

Reclining Woman, 1927

cast concrete, 25 in (63.5 cm) long, The Moore Danowski Trust, Perry Green, England

This simplified figure shows the beginning of Moore's interest in abstraction. His reclining figures never had slender limbs or details such as hair or nails. These details would have distracted from the impact of the solid forms. In later years, the heads would often be reduced to shapes without eyes, a nose, or a mouth.

"Fry opened the way to other books and to the reali[z]ation of the British Museum. That was really the beginning."

Henry Moore

A Taste of Europe

▲ A Portland stone quarry. Moore's *West Wind* (opposite) was carved from Portland Stone.

PORTLAND STONE

Portland is an island off the coast of Dorset in southern England. Quarrying for Portland stone, which is a type of limestone, dates back to the 12th century. It became popular in the 17th century when Sir Christopher Wren (1632-1723) chose Portland stone for the rebuilding of London after the Great Fire of 1666. John Nash (1752-1835) also used it for the construction of Buckingham Palace in the 19th century. Today Portland stone remains a popular material for all types of building, from large business developments to historic restorations and private homes.

In 1922, Moore visited Paris to view the work of the artist Paul Cézanne. He returned to London inspired by what he had seen. In 1924 he began teaching sculpture at the Royal College of Art (RCA). Teaching supported Moore financially for many years until he could earn enough from the sale of his art.

In 1925, Moore took time off to travel to Paris and Italy. During his trip Moore saw the great works of the Old Masters, including his favorite Michelangelo.

STYLE DILEMMA

Moore loved the classical work he had seen in Europe but he still felt drawn to primitive sculpture. After returning to London, he continued using his primitive style and began exhibiting his work. His first solo show was at the Warren Gallery in London in 1928.

LANDMARK YEAR

Moore met two key people in 1928 — the art critic Herbert Read (1893-1968), who became a life-long friend and supporter, and a young Russian student, Irina Radetsky, Moore's future wife. He also began his first commission, *West Wind* (opposite), for the London Transport Headquarters.

▶ *Rondanini Pietà*, 1552-64, Michelangelo. Moore admired this piece saying, "I don't know of any other single work of art by anyone that is more poignant, more moving."

TIMELINE ▶

1922	1923	1924	1925	1928
Moore sees Cézanne's work in Paris.	Moore sells his first piece of work as a professional artist.	Moore holds his first exhibition of carvings in London. He becomes sculpture instructor at the Royal College of Art.	He wins a travel scholarship to Italy, then returns to teach at the RCA. He investigates different types of stone at the Geological Society.	Moore has his first solo show at the Warren Gallery, London. He meets Herbert Read and Irina Radetsky. He begins work on *West Wind*.

West Wind, 1928–29

Portland stone, 96 in (244 cm) long, London Transport Headquarters, St. James's Park Underground Station, London, England

This type of one-sided sculpture that sticks out slightly from the wall is called a "relief" sculpture.
Moore's sculpture was one of four reliefs carved for this building. Together they symbolize the four winds.
The floating movement of his figure's limbs suggests the dynamic power of the weather. Moore decided
that the figure should be female since the west wind is generally a gentler wind.

*"Sculpture in stone should look honestly like stone...
to make it look like flesh and blood, hair and dimples
is coming down to the level of stage conjurer."*

Henry Moore

Direct Carving

Many sculptors work by making clay models and then casting them in metal. However, for much of his career, Moore chose to concentrate on a different method – carving directly into stone or wood.

TRUTH TO MATERIAL

Direct carving was considered risky – one slip of the chisel and the entire piece would be ruined. The phrase "truth to material" was often used to describe this process because it was as though artists were working with nature, not against it. Some artists even believed that the sculpture was already in the stone and that they were merely uncovering it.

"I liked the fact that you begin with the block and have to find the sculpture that is inside. You have to overcome the resistance of the material by sheer determination and hard work."

Henry Moore

In many ways Moore followed the thinking of artist Pablo Picasso (1881-1973) who said that he was not inventing his pictures but uncovering something that had always existed in the human mind. As he put it, "I do not seek, I find."

JACOB EPSTEIN

The sculptor Jacob Epstein (1880-1959), whom Moore admired, also practiced direct carving. He was born in New York and began drawing while working in a bronze foundry. In 1902, he went to study art in Paris, where he often visited the Louvre. The ancient and primitive sculpture he saw there was a continuing influence on his work.

◄ *Night*, 1928-29, Jacob Epstein.
This is one of two figures Epstein carved for the same building as Moore's *West Wind* (page 13). Members of the public found Epstein's figures offensive and vandalized them.

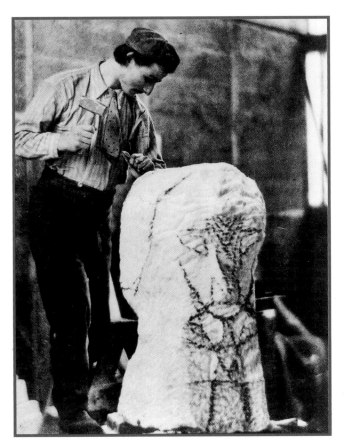

HENRI GAUDIER-BRZESKA

Moore was also influenced by a French sculptor who had moved to London in 1911. Gaudier-Brzeska (1891-1915) was considered a young genius but was tragically killed at age 23 while fighting for the French army.

Moore had first discovered Gaudier-Brzeska's work while he was a student at the Royal College of Art. Although the two never met, Gaudier-Brzeska inspired Moore to break away from traditional sculptural methods. Gaudier-Brzeska also admired Epstein, calling him "the foremost in the small number of good sculptors in Europe."

◀ The young Henri Gaudier-Brzeska at work on *Head of Ezra Pound*, 1914, using the direct carving technique.

"Sculptural energy is the mountain."

Henri Gaudier-Brzeska

ERIC GILL

Eric Gill (1882-1940) was a skilled wood carver, illustrator, sculptor, and typeface designer. He produced many carvings for public buildings, including *The Stations of the Cross* in Westminster Cathedral and, with Moore, a wind piece for the London Transport Headquarters. He is perhaps best known internationally for his typeface Gill Sans, which was based on a font designed in 1916 for London Underground signs.

▶ *Stations of the Cross, IV. Jesus Meets His Mother*, 1918, Eric Gill. This is one of a series of reliefs carved for Westminster Cathedral.

BENEDICTA TU IN MULIERIBUS

IV. JESUS MEETS HIS MOTHER

This paragraph is set in Gill Sans. "Sans" is short for "sans serif" which means without serif. Serifs are the tiny bars across the end of a letter's stroke in typefaces such as the one used for the quotations in this book.

Established Artist

In 1928, the influential art critic Herbert Read wrote one of the first major articles on Moore's work. It was very supportive and backed up Moore's opinions on truth to material and direct carving.

By now Moore's sculptures were becoming widely recognized. They were regularly exhibited in London and also began selling abroad. Moore was gaining confidence and themes began developing in his work.

A LIFE-LONG THEME

Moore was impressed by a limestone carving of the ancient Mexican rain spirit, Chacmool. Moore had seen a picture of it in a German magazine and a plaster copy of it in Paris.

The reclining figure became a life-long obsession for Moore. It was both classical and primitive and enabled Moore to experiment with shape and explore different ways of sculpting.

▼ **An example of a *Chacmool* from Mexico, c. 12th century A.D.**
Moore spoke of the Chacmool's "stillness and alertness, a sense of readiness – and the whole presence of it."

RECLINING FIGURES

Reclining figures have a long tradition in art, from primitive and classical sculpture to the paintings of Diego Velázquez (1599-1660), Jean Ingres (1780-1867), Gustave Courbet (1819-77), and Paul Gauguin. During the Renaissance they were used to illustrate the Greek goddess Venus of classical mythology. Later artists used them to explore themes linked to nature. By Moore's time, many Modernist artists were portraying the female nude as strong, powerful, and in control.

For sculptors working in stone, the reclining nude also has a practical aspect – stone has weak points and a standing figure might break at the ankles or neck.

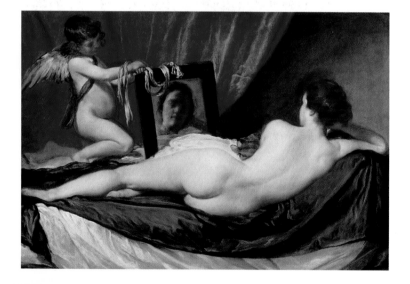

◄ *Venus at Her Mirror*, **1644-48, Diego Velázquez.** Here Venus reclines on her side, spanning the length of the canvas.

TIMELINE ▶

May 1929	July 1929	1930
Moore completes his first reclining figure clearly showing the influence of the ancient Mexican rain spirit *Chacmool*. This includes his first use of a hole in his sculpture.	Moore marries Irina. The couple move to Hampstead and become friends with an up-and-coming group of artists.	Moore joins an avant-garde artists' group, Seven and Five. He exhibits work in the British Pavilion at the Venice Biennale, an important international art show.

Reclining Figure, 1929

brown Hornton stone, 33 ¹/2 in (85 cm) long, Leeds Museums and Galleries, Leeds, England

This figure was Moore's first real reference to the Mexican *Chacmool*. It lies at a similar angle, head raised, and knees bent, and has the same sense of heaviness. Like the *Chacmool*, it confronts the viewer with an inquisitive look. It has a much more striking presence than the *Reclining Woman* Moore carved two years earlier (see page 11). Moore made a number of female reclining figures, both nude and dressed in stone-carved drapery. He only sculpted one reclining male figure, although it no longer exists.

"Henry Moore, in virtue of his sureness and consistency, springs straight to the head of the modern movement in England."

Herbert Read, the Listener magazine, 1928

The Hampstead set

Moore married Irina Radetsky in 1929, and shortly afterwards they moved to Hampstead, north London. Around the same time, political problems in Europe were driving many artists and writers to London so that it rivalled Paris as the centre of the art world.

Hampstead became a base for this creative energy. Moore's neighbours included Barbara Hepworth, Herbert Read, painter Ben Nicholson (1894-1982) and sculptors John Skeaping (1901-80) and the Russian Naum Gabo (1890-1977). They went on holiday together and formed artists' groups such as *Seven and Five* and *Unit One*. In 1930 Moore was invited to represent British sculpture at the prestigious Venice Biennale alongside Jacob Epstein and John Skeaping.

▲ Henry and Irina Moore on their wedding day, 29 July 1929. Moore made many sketches of Irina as they settled into their new life together among the Bohemian intellectuals of Hampstead.

UNIT ONE

The elite, avant-garde artists' group *Unit One* was established in 1933 and was based at the Mayor Gallery in London. Moore joined the group that year along with painters Paul Nash (1889-1946) and Edward Burra (1905-76), and architect Wells Coates (1895-1958).

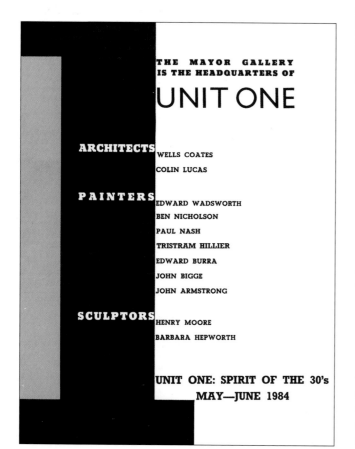

THE MAYOR GALLERY
IS THE HEADQUARTERS OF

UNIT ONE

ARCHITECTS
WELLS COATES
COLIN LUCAS

PAINTERS
EDWARD WADSWORTH
BEN NICHOLSON
PAUL NASH
TRISTRAM HILLIER
EDWARD BURRA
JOHN BIGGE
JOHN ARMSTRONG

SCULPTORS
HENRY MOORE
BARBARA HEPWORTH

UNIT ONE: SPIRIT OF THE 30's
MAY—JUNE 1984

◀ Catalogue from a 1984 exhibition celebrating the work of *Unit One* and held at the same gallery as the first *Unit One* exhibition of 1933. The cover is typical of 1930s' design when it would have been considered very modern, reflecting the avante-garde nature of the group.

The *Unit One* artists announced in *The Times* that they promoted 'the expression of a truly contemporary spirit' – in other words, creating art and architecture with a very up-to-date feel. In 1933, to coincide with the publication of Read's book *Art Now*, the Mayor gallery held an exhibition with works by *Unit One* artists Moore, Hepworth and Nicholson alongside distinguished European artists.

▲ On holiday at Happisburgh, Norfolk, 1931. From left to right: artist Ivon Hitchens (1893-1979), Irina Moore, Henry Moore, Barbara Hepworth, Ben Nicholson and friend Mary Jenkins.

BARBARA HEPWORTH

Like Moore, Barbara Hepworth (1903-75) was born in Yorkshire and studied at the Leeds School of Art and the Royal College of Art in London. While living in Hampstead, she developed a strong working relationship with Moore and their sculptures show many similarities. They were once overheard arguing over which of them was copying the other! They shared an interest in landscape, abstraction, truth to material and direct carving, but Hepworth's work is considered more serene and classical than Moore's.

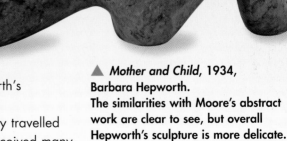

▲ *Mother and Child*, 1934, Barbara Hepworth.
The similarities with Moore's abstract work are clear to see, but overall Hepworth's sculpture is more delicate.

Hepworth was married to Ben Nicholson, and together they travelled around Europe visiting important abstract artists. Barbara received many public commissions and awards throughout her career, including the Grand Prix at the São Paulo Biennale in 1959 and Dame Commander of the British Empire in 1965. She died in a house fire in 1975.

The Surreal Thirties

In 1931, Moore resigned from the Royal College of Art after a newspaper article about his work caused a public scandal. However, it was only a brief setback. Soon afterward Moore started a sculpture department at Chelsea College of Art in London.

SURREALISM

In London at this time, artists were becoming interested in a movement called Surrealism that began in Europe in the early 1920s. Surrealists such as Salvador Dali (1904-89) based their art on images from the unconscious mind and dreams. As a result, this type of art was often hard to make sense of.

Although Moore agreed with some of the Surrealists' ideas, he was never entirely associated with them. He would pick and choose aspects of the movement, such as imagination and inventiveness, but preferred to control how his sculpture looked instead of letting his subconscious mind take over.

▲ Government militia fight in the streets of Barcelona during the Spanish Civil War, 1936.

THE SPANISH CIVIL WAR

In 1936, civil war broke out in Spain. An extreme right-wing group called the Fascists were fighting viciously for control of the country. Three years later they finally declared victory. Fascist General Franco was made Spain's head of state, and remained leader, or dictator, until his death in 1975.

Many artists and writers wanted to fight against the Fascists. Some actually fought, such as the writer George Orwell (1903-50), while others, such as Ernest Hemingway (1899-1961) and W.H. Auden (1907-73), drove ambulances or helped in other ways. Moore signed the manifesto of the English Surrealist Group against British non-intervention in Spain and tried to go there, but his request for a travel permit was rejected.

▲ Photograph of the International Surrealist Exhibition at the New Burlington Galleries, London, 1936. Moore showed work at this event including *Reclining Figure*, 1933 (center stand) and *Figure*, 1933-34 (far right stand).

TIMELINE ▶

1932	1933	1934	1935	1936
Moore is appointed head of the new sculpture department at Chelsea College of Art.	Moore joins avant-garde group Unit One.	The Moores make a trip to Spain, visiting Barcelona, Madrid, Toledo, and Altamira.	Moore has an exhibition of drawings at the Zwemmer Gallery in London.	The Spanish Civil War breaks out. Moore signs the manifesto of the English Surrealist Group against British non-intervention in Spain.

Two Seated Women, 1934

charcoal, watercolor, pen and ink, crayon on cream medium-weight wove paper,
14 1/2 x 21 2/3 in (37 x 55 cm), The Henry Moore Foundation, Perry Green, England

**Moore's inventiveness with the human form was close to that of the Surrealists.
They created images that would not be seen in reality. In this drawing, Moore distorts
the human figures into fantastic shapes so that they are part biology, part geometry.**

*"There are universal shapes to which everybody is subconsciously
conditioned and to which they can respond if their conscious
mind does not shut them off."*

Henry Moore

Abstract forms

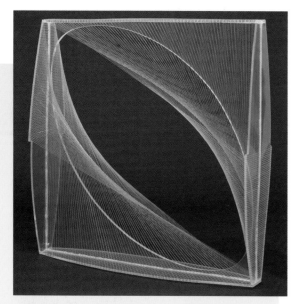

▲ *Linear Construction No. 1*, 1942-3, Naum Gabo. From his initial sketches, Gabo went on to construct many stringed sculptures like this one.

THE ART OF CONSTRUCTION

Other artists also worked from scientific and mathematical models. Hepworth had started to experiment with stringed sculpture around the same time, and the Russian artist Naum Gabo (1890-1977) – now also living in Hampstead – made drawings of stringed objects as early as 1933. In Russia in 1920, Gabo and his brother Antoine Pevsner (1886-1962) had issued a 'constructivist manifesto'. They aimed to move away from traditional sculptural methods, such as stone carving, and to explore space with new forms and materials. They wanted to create a classless society that used architecture and technology to make everyone equal.

While Moore was experimenting with Surrealist ideas, he was also developing his abstract style. During the 1930s his work became increasingly simplified and removed from reality. Even so, Moore insisted that it was as true to nature as lifelike art. He was simply reducing objects to their simplest form, or building them up from basic shapes.

STRINGED SCULPTURE

On a visit to London's Science Museum, Moore came across mathematical models that used string or nylon to create a line. When he incorporated these into his own sculptures, they opened up his blocky forms, allowing light through. Moore was excited by 'the ability to look through the strings as with a bird cage and to see one form within another'.

'There is just as much shape in a hole as a lump.'

Henry Moore

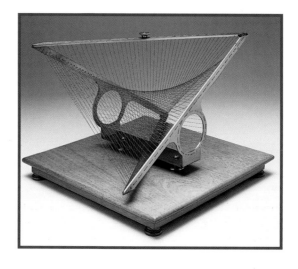

◄ An example of a mathematical model from the Science Museum, London.

TIMELINE ▶

1937	1938	1939	1940
Moore visits Picasso's studio in Paris to see the famous painting *Guernica*. He produces his first stringed sculpture.	Moore is refused a permit to visit Spain. He starts to use modelling and casting as well as direct carving. He participates in the International Exhibition of Abstract Art at the Stedelijk Museum, Amsterdam.	Moore resigns from the Chelsea College of Art. World War II begins.	Moore takes over Hepworth's studio in Hampstead.

Bird Basket, 1939

lignum vitae and string 42 cm long The Henry Moore Foundation, Perry Green

Moore wrote: 'It is called the *Bird Basket* because it has the handle of a basket over the top and strings to show the little inner piece as a bird inside a cage – at one end is the head and at the other the tail.' Moore uses string just as a painter would use a brush to draw a line. The line stands out against the solid form of the wood and emphasises the three-dimensional space.

'They think that abstraction means getting away from reality and it often means precisely the opposite – that you are getting closer to it... nearer to an emotional understanding.'

Henry Moore

War Artist

While Moore was growing increasingly successful, Europe was spiraling into full-scale war. At 11:15 A.M. on Sunday, September 3, 1939, the British Prime Minister Neville Chamberlain announced that Britain was at war with Germany.

Moore had fought in World War I but was now too old to be drafted into the army. He initially turned down an invitation to be an official war artist, thinking he could be more useful as a precision tool maker – but then events around him persuaded him to change his mind. During the months of waiting for a training place, he made drawings of people taking shelter from the air raids in London. The official bomb shelters were not big enough so people took shelter on the platforms of underground, or subway, stations.

▲ Moore revisited the London Underground in September of 1943 to film *Out of Chaos*, a documentary about war artists which also included Paul Nash and Stanley Spencer.

"I saw people lying on the platforms at all the stations we stopped at… I had never seen so many reclining figures, and even the train tunnels seemed to be like the holes in my sculpture."

Henry Moore

◀ *Tube Shelter Perspective: The Liverpool Street Extension*, 1941, Henry Moore. The scratchy effect comes from using pen, chalk, and paint together. It gives the drawing a ghostly, anxious feel, reflecting the mood in the shelters during air raids.

AN OFFICIAL PROJECT

The official war artists project was first set up by the British government during World War I. It began in 1916 as a way of getting messages to the public and recording events in the war. Many great artists were involved, including painters Paul Nash (1889-1946), John Singer Sargent (1856-1925), and Stanley Spencer (1891-1959). On the outbreak of World War II, the War Artists' Advisory Committee began to commission artists in a similar way.

> *"It seemed a good way of preventing artists being killed."*
>
> *Kenneth Clark, War Artists' Advisory Committee*

MOORE FOR MORALE

When the Committee saw Moore's shelter drawings they immediately asked him to record the Blitz, or German air raid, in London. The work would be exhibited around the country to boost morale. Moore changed his mind and became an official war artist, earning enough to survive without teaching for the first time.

THE UNDERGROUND ARMY

In 1942, Moore began another drawing project. He returned to Castleford to sketch the coal miners, known as the Underground Army. Moore found this hard. He preferred to draw the female form and found the harsh movements of the pit men too different from his usual still subjects.

THE LONDON BLITZ

In 1940 the German air force bombed British airfields and radar stations in preparation for the invasion of England. The invasion never happened. Instead, Hitler ordered the destruction of London by air raids. On September 7, 1940, German planes bombed the capital for 12 hours. This intense attack, known as the Blitz, continued for months. Whole areas of London were destroyed. The Blitz ended on May 11, 1941, when Hitler called off the raids in order to move his bombers east and invade Russia.

The Blitz affected Moore directly. In 1940, a bomb fell close to his home in Hampstead, destroying the doors and windows. Soon afterward, another blast cut off the gas and water supplies. The Moores decided to leave the city and move to a farmhouse called Hoglands in Perry Green, England. This was a turning point for Moore. He saw his work in the open countryside for the first time.

▲ **Families trying to recover from the devastation of their homes after the Blitz, London, 1940-41.**

Family and fame

The Festival of Britain took place between May and September 1951. After the hardship of the war years, the Festival aimed to raise the nation's spirits and promote British art, design and industry. Moore created a reclining figure especially for the event. The South Bank Exhibition and the Festival Pleasure Gardens in Battersea were the main London venues, but there were celebrations all over Britain. People, still affected by shortages and rationing arising from the war, were offered fun and education with theatre, dance, music, art exhibitions, firework displays, cafés and entertaining side-shows. Post-war freedom was to be enjoyed by everyone.

▲ *Reclining Figure: Festival*, 1951, on display at London's South Bank. This was one of the first pieces in which Moore tried to make the gaps and spaces as important as the bronze itself. The figure is almost half air.

World War II finally ended in 1945 and Europe started rebuilding after the devastation. Families were reunited and desperately wanted to return to normality.

On 7 March 1946, Moore's only child Mary was born. Britain itself was being reborn, and this led to the commissioning of large public sculptures in new towns throughout southern England. One of these was Moore's *Family Group* (opposite).

▲ Moore at home with his daughter Mary, Easter 1951.

BRANCHING OUT

By now Moore was realising that the idea of 'truth to material' could also be applied to bronze. What's more, he could do things with bronze that he couldn't do with stone. He could cast upright figures without the ankles snapping and make them top heavy. Bronze would also last better outdoors.

This new development coincided with Moore's growing international success. In 1943, he had had his first solo exhibition abroad – in New York. This was followed by a travelling retrospective which opened in 1946. In 1948, Moore represented Britain at the Venice Biennale and won the International Prize for Sculpture for his one-man show.

TIMELINE ▶

1944	1945	1946	1948	1949	1951
Moore's mother dies.	World War II ends.	Birth of Moore's only child, Mary.	Moore has a solo show at the Venice Biennale. He wins the International Prize for Sculpture.	Moore holds an exhibition at the Palais des Beaux-Arts, Brussels, which then travels (1948-51) to Paris, Amsterdam, Hamburg, Düsseldorf, Berne and Athens.	Moore visits Greece and its classical ruins. He participates in the Festival of Britain and has a restrospective at the Tate Gallery.

Family Group, 1948–9
bronze 152 cm high Tate, London
Moore sculpted many family groups which were just right for the optimistic atmosphere
that developed after the war. They symbolised unity and hope for the future.

Royal Recognition

By the 1950s Moore was recognized worldwide as an influential figure. He was offered a knighthood by King George VI in 1950, but refused it. He felt it might cut him off from his fellow artists.

Moore's days of causing outrage with his modern approach and ideas were over. Now his work was accepted and he became a respected member of established art societies.

TO SCOTLAND

Moore had many wealthy supporters, one of which was Sir William Keswick. On a visit to Moore's house, Keswick saw the large bronze sculpture *King and Queen* (opposite) on the lawn outside and decided that he wanted it for his own estate at Glenkiln in Scotland.

> *"It's a most glorious place for it, very wild and surprisingly right."*
>
> *Henry Moore*

▲ Queen Elizabeth II at her coronation, 1953.

▲ Moore (seated fourth from the right) with other members of the Order of Merit at Buckingham Palace, 1972.

THE CORONATION

It is likely that Moore's idea for *King and Queen* stemmed from the excitement leading up to the coronation of Elizabeth II. Elizabeth was crowned Queen of England on June 2, 1953, following the death of her father George VI in February of 1952.

The build-up to the ceremony was very public, and it was the first royal event to be televised. Some thought that this was undignified, but an estimated 20 million people saw the young Queen crowned.

Moore met Elizabeth in person. In 1955 she made him a Companion of Honour and in 1963 awarded him the Order of Merit.

TIMELINE ▶

1952	1953	1954	1955
Moore has exhibitions in Sweden, South Africa, Austria, and the Netherlands.	Moore is awarded the International Sculpture Prize at the second São Paulo Biennale. He travels to Brazil and Mexico.	Moore's international reputation continues to grow.	Moore is made a Companion of Honour by Queen Elizabeth II. He becomes a Trustee of the National Gallery.

King and Queen, 1952–53

bronze, 64 $^1/_2$ x 54 $^1/_3$ x 33 $^1/_4$ in (164 x 138 x 84.5 cm), Keswick Estate, Glenkiln, Dumfriesshire, Scotland

The two figures in this sculpture sit serenely in the Scottish countryside. They stare out over the water of the loch in a regal and dignified pose.

"I was reading stories to Mary, my six-year-old daughter, every night, and most of them were about kings and queens and princesses."

Henry Moore

Giant commissions

▲ Gargoyles high up on the walls of Notre Dame cathedral stare down on the city of Paris far below them.

SCULPTURE TO LOOK UP TO

There have been sculptures around the tops of buildings for centuries. In medieval times builders made gargoyles, which were often ornamental spouts, designed to carry rainwater away from roofs.

Gargoyles were carved to look like animals or human faces, usually imaginative and often ugly or frightening. They can still be seen today on many churches. Moore had made copies of gargoyles in Leeds while he was a student.

There are many myths about gargoyles. They are supposed to stand guard and ward off unwanted spirits and other creatures, or come alive at night when everyone's asleep and protect the church. Winged gargoyles are said to fly round the whole village or town and return to their places when the sun comes up.

During the 1950s Moore started receiving large commissions from big businesses. He could now impress the public more than ever. His success enabled him to hire assistants – young sculptors such as Anthony Caro (b.1924) – to help him.

THE TIME-LIFE SCREEN

A new building on Bond Street in London had just been built for the *Time-Life Magazine* company. Its owners wanted it to reflect British creative talent, so they invited Moore to contribute.

Moore installed one of his reclining figures in the third floor garden terrace, and then created a huge screen that went around the four sides of the top of the building. He planned this vast sculpture – and almost all from then on – using small scale models called maquettes.

▲ *Time-Life Screen: Maquette No.1*, 1952, Henry Moore. Maquettes are like 3-D sketches. They enabled Moore to plan large sculptures without having to work life-size. His assistants would help enlarge the final maquettes. Moore said: 'Always in my mind, though, in making these little ideas, is the eventual sculpture which may be ten or twelve times the size of the maquette that I hold in my hand.'

TIMELINE ▶

1957	1959	1960
Moore shows work at the Fourth International Exhibition of Sculpture in the Open Air, London.	Moore receives another cascade of awards and has many exhibitions worldwide.	Many German towns commission large bronzes by Moore as public sculptures. Alice Gostick, Moore's pottery teacher, dies.

Time-Life Screen, 1952-3

Portland stone 808 cm long Pearl Assurance, Time-Life Building, London

Moore wanted the four large sculptures to be on a turntable so that they could be rotated each month, but this was thought too dangerous. Instead, he made the carvings three dimensional rather than in relief, so that the overall effect was of figures embedded in the screens. There were holes incorporated into the design, so that the passer-by could see it was sculpture and not part of the building.

'There is a right physical size for every idea.'

Henry Moore

A Collector of Objects

▲ Moore's collection of objects in the sitting room at Hoglands, 1966.

The technique of etching is a painstaking process. The artist scratches a picture onto a highly polished sheet of copper which has been coated with an acid-resistant substance, known as "ground." The copper is then immersed in a bath of acid which "bites" into the scratched lines. Next it is covered with ink, then cleaned to leave ink in the grooves only. The plate is then placed on an etching press and covered with a sheet of heavy, damp paper. The press forces the paper into the ink-filled grooves and the image is then transferred onto the paper.

During his lifetime, Moore collected many objects and artworks. The sitting room at Hoglands was full of ancient sculpture, bones, and stones, as well as 19th-century paintings. Works by his British contemporaries, such as Paul Nash and Ben Nicholson, were elsewhere in the house.

SKULLS AND BONES

It would be hard for us to tell the difference between the natural and the man-made things in Moore's collection. For Moore every piece had a meaning, especially an elephant skull he had been given. Not only did this inspire the sculpture *Atom Piece*, but it also led Moore to take up etching.

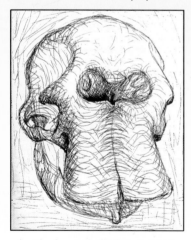

▲ *Elephant Skull Plate I*, 1969. Moore's etched lines follow the curving, 3-D form of the skull.

▲ Moore working on an etching plate with the elephant skull in his studio at Hoglands, 1970.

TIMELINE ▶

1961	1963	1964
Moore is elected a member of the American Academy of Art and Letters. He exhibits at the Scottish National Gallery of Modern Art in Edinburgh, Scotland.	Moore takes up etching. He receives the Order of Merit from Queen Elizabeth II.	Moore is appointed a member of the Arts Council of Great Britain and reappointed as a Trustee of the National Gallery.

Atom Piece, 1965

bronze, 48 in (122cm) high,
Didrichsen Art Museum,
Helsinki, Finland

Here, Moore takes the
shape of the elephant
skull and transforms it
into a modern work
of art that reflects
the "atomic age."
The smooth,
rounded form
reminded scientists
of "mushroom
clouds emanating
from an atomic
explosion."

Marble Marvels

THE CHANGING ART WORLD

In 1968, the Tate Gallery, London, held a retrospective of Moore's work. This was a time when youth culture was on the rise, students were rebelling, and there were student riots in many countries. Moore's old assistant Anthony Caro was now rivaling the popularity of his master. It was a decade of experimental sculpture and conceptual art, which meant that a thought often counted for more than an object. An artwork could be a walk through the countryside or a sentence on a wall. One artist, Bruce McLean (b.1944), exhibited photographs of himself pretending to be Moore's reclining figures.

▲ *Pose Work for Plinths 3*, 1971, Bruce McLean. McLean was pointing out that art was no longer just about sculpture and painting.

In 1965, Moore bought a house near the Carrara marble quarries in Italy. From there, he could easily access the marble and work on his large public sculptures nearby. Moore was increasingly interested in marble and its potential for creating smooth, curvaceous forms. It also gave him a link to the great classical sculptors he admired. Michelangelo had used the same source of marble for his own work.

▲ Moore at the Henraux marble quarry in the Carrara Mountains, Italy, not far from his villa. Moore would spend summer mornings working here since the marble slabs were too heavy to take to his studio.

MOTHER AND CHILD

Mother and Child is an example of how Moore used the natural qualities of marble to make his work expressive. Here, the red veins in the stone run between the two figures, giving them life and suggesting a bond between them. At the same time, the polished curves remind us of the softness of the human body. Throughout his career, Moore was obsessed with the "mother and child" theme. Among other things, it reflected the subject matter of many paintings and sculptures by the Old Masters.

TIMELINE ▶

1965	1967	1968
Moore buys a summer house in Italy. He also visits New York for the installation of a *Reclining Figure* at the Lincoln Center.	Replicas of Moore's work are used in a set for the opera *Don Giovanni* in Italy. Moore visits Canada. He is elected Fellow of the British Academy.	Moore has a retrospective at the Tate Gallery, to coincide with his 70th birthday. He is created Honorary Doctor by the Royal College of Art, London.

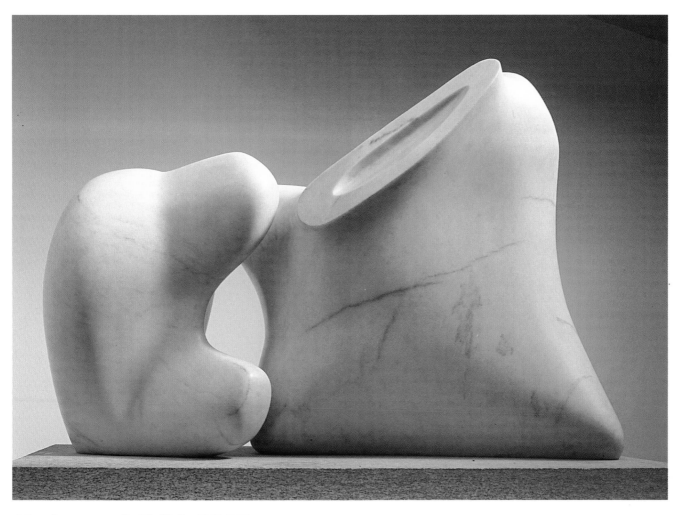

Mother and Child, 1967

rosa aurora marble, 51 $^1/_2$ in (130.8 cm) long, The Henry Moore Foundation, Perry Green, England

Moore is considered a "humanist" artist because he dealt with familiar themes that we have all experienced. In this piece, he portrays the relationship between mother and child in an abstract way – the contact between the large form and small form gives a feeling of protection. Perhaps Moore was inspired by the relationship he had with his own mother.

"It has been a universal theme from the beginning of time ... I discovered, when drawing, I could turn every little scribble, blot or smudge into a Mother and Child."

Henry Moore

Home and Away

▲ *Knife Edge Mirror Two-Piece*, 1977-78, stands outside the National Gallery of Art in Washington, D.C. Moore made this piece nearly 26 feet (8 m) high so that from a distance it didn't look like a person going into the gallery.

CASTING IN BRONZE

There are two main methods of bronze casting: "sand casting" and "lost wax casting." Moore used wax, and for a while did it himself with the help of two assistants. Most of the time he had his casting done at professional foundries.

In the lost wax method, a wax replica is made of the artist's original work (which is usually a plaster or clay model). This replica is covered with "grog" – a mixture of water, plaster, and ground-up pottery – which sets hard around the wax. The mold is then baked in a kiln. The heat melts the wax, which runs out of a hole left in the mold. Molten bronze is poured in through the hole so that it fills the space left by the "lost" wax. The final piece is then hand-finished to smooth off any rough areas.

By the time Moore reached his 70s, his art was on display all over the world. His age did not limit his traveling or the size of his sculptures at all. In between trips abroad, Moore kept working at Hoglands.

SCALE AND STATURE

Moore had separate studios for different ways of working, including maquettes, printmaking, and a huge outdoor studio for large sculpture. By this stage in his life, he was wealthy enough to be extravagant with scale and material. Most of his later works were massive monuments cast in bronze.

Sheep Piece (opposite) was one of these huge sculptures. Moore had started drawing sheep during preparations for a big exhibition in Florence in 1972. There were so many people at the exhibition that he retreated to a room facing fields where his neighbor's sheep grazed. The sheep wandered up close to the window and Moore began to draw them.

◀ *Head*, 1972, page 45 from *Sheep Sketchbook*, Henry Moore. Moore kept a sketchbook of his many sheep drawings.

TIMELINE ▶

1972	1974	1975	1976
The Henry Moore Trust is set up. Moore receives more honors and holds more major exhibitions, including a large retrospective in Florence, Italy.	The Henry Moore Sculpture Centre is opened in Ontario, Canada.	Barbara Hepworth dies in a fire.	There is an exhibition of war drawings at the Imperial War Museum, including a selection by Moore.

Sheep Piece, 1971-72

bronze, 216 1/2 in (550 cm) tall, The Henry Moore Foundation, Perry Green, England

Moore placed many of his sculptures in the countryside because he thought the open sky made a dramatic background. *Sheep Piece* was made to stand in a field where his neighbors' lambs could play around it. It became a shelter for the sheep. Moore preferred his sculpture to be among sheep rather than cows or horses because their small size enhanced the impressive scale of his work.

"At first I saw them as rather shapeless balls of wool with a head and four legs. Then I began to reali[z]e that underneath all that wool was a body, which moved in its own way, and that each sheep had its individual character."

Henry Moore

The Last Years

Moore had an extremely long and successful career as an artist, and outlived many of his friends. He had become a grandfather, traveled the globe, and received many awards. He had always been ambitious and seemed to have followed the very best path for a world renowned sculptor.

By the end of his life, Moore's work was visible in many parts of the world and he had dozens of public sculptures in the United States.

FINAL FEATS

In his later years, Moore suffered from arthritis and ill health, and became less productive. Nevertheless, work still went on at Hoglands. Moore had kept many old maquettes from previous decades, and throughout the 1980s his assistants made new casts from them. Moore continued to draw, and his work still made its mark elsewhere. In 1982, the Henry Moore Centre for the Study of Sculpture opened in Leeds.

Moore died on August 31, 1986, at the age of 88.

▲ Toward the end of his life, Moore spent much of his time drawing at home.

A memorial service was held at Westminster Abbey in London. His wife, Irina, died two years later.

CÉZANNE'S BATHERS

A favorite theme for Moore's late drawings was Paul Cézanne's paintings of bathers. Cézanne was said to be a forerunner of an art style called Cubism because he reduced nature to basic geometric shapes. He also used colors to create different moods.

Moore had first seen Cézanne's *Bathers* in Paris when he was a student. There is a noticeable similarity between Cézanne's paintings of curvaceous bodies and Moore's drawn and sculpted figures.

◄ *Large Bathers,*1899-1906, Paul Cézanne. Cézanne distorted natural forms to suit his own artistic purpose.

TIMELINE ▶

1977	1979	1982	August 31, 1986
The Henry Moore Foundation is established in Perry Green. Moore's grandson Gus is born.	Moore's "Mother and Child" theme becomes dominant. He gets arthritis and has to start working on a smaller scale.	Henry Moore Centre for the Study of Sculpture opens in Leeds. A *Reclining Figure* that Moore carved from elmwood in 1946 sells for $1,000,000 at an auction in New York.	Henry Moore dies.

Study After Cézanne's "Bathers," 1980

carbon line, wax crayon, watercolor, chalk, and chinagraph on heavyweight wove paper, 9 4/5 x 5 1/3 in (25 x 13.7 cm),
The Henry Moore Foundation, Perry Green, England

Moore's drawings have the same solidity as his monumental sculptures. It is as though he has turned
Cézanne's painted figures into a drawing of stone carvings. Neither Cézanne nor Moore was interested
in portraying the human body in perfect proportion. Their figures have a life of their own which comes
from the sensitive and energetic use of the artist's chosen material.

*"I find in all the artists that I admire most a disturbing element,
a distortion, giving evidence of a struggle… In great art, this
conflict is hidden, it is unresolved. All that is bursting with
energy is disturbing – not perfect."*

Henry Moore

Moore's Legacy

Moore had a profound effect on the way sculpture is presented to the public today. One of the most revolutionary things about him was his desire to place work out in the open. Most artists preferred to show art in galleries, where attention was focused on it. Sculpture outside the gallery tended to be limited to historical monuments of famous generals or politicians. Moore changed all this and had financial backing.

During the 1980s, more companies and governments around the world invested in public art and sculpture. These works of art are now popular landmarks in the towns and cities of many countries.

FIGURES IN LANDSCAPE

A large number of artists have been influenced by Moore's work with the figure in landscape. They include Antony Gormley (b.1950), whose *Angel of the North* (below) stands 66 feet (20 m) tall with a wingspan of 171 feet (52 m). It towers against the sky in northeast England and can be seen for miles around. Its roadside position is passed by about 90,000 vehicles every day.

"The hilltop site is important and has the feeling of being a megalithic mound."

Antony Gormley

◀ **Angel of the North, 1998, Antony Gormley.** This striking figure stands on the remains of an old mine in Northeast England. It is a powerful symbol of humanity and the achievements of the industrial age. As Gormley put it, "When you think of the mining that was done underneath the site, there is a poetic resonance. Men worked beneath the surface in the dark. Now, in the light, there is a celebration of this industry."

CITY SCULPTURE

French artist Niki de Saint Phalle (1930-2002) made brightly colored, oversized figures for cityscapes and sculpture gardens. She collaborated with the Swiss artist Jean Tinguely (1925-91) to create a landmark fountain for the plaza of the Pompidou Centre in Paris.

> *"Life… is never the way one imagines it."*
>
> Niki de Saint Phalle

▲ *Igor Stravinsky Fountain*, **completed 1983, Niki de Saint Phalle and Jean Tinguely.** This fountain stands outside the Pompidou Centre in Paris. Inspired by the music of composer Igor Stravinsky, the fun rotating figures contrast brilliantly with the serious industrial look of the building.

THE HENRY MOORE FOUNDATION

Moore set up the Henry Moore Foundation at Perry Green in 1977, in order to "advance the education of the public by the promotion of their appreciation of the fine arts," especially the works of Henry Moore.

The Foundation runs the Henry Moore Institute in Leeds, collaborates with artists and galleries to show new work, and awards grants in support of artists' projects. It also owns the largest collection of Moore's work, most of which is displayed in the buildings and grounds of the artist's estate.

BIOMORPHIC DESIGN

▼ **The curvaceous design of this car is an example of modern biomorphic design.**

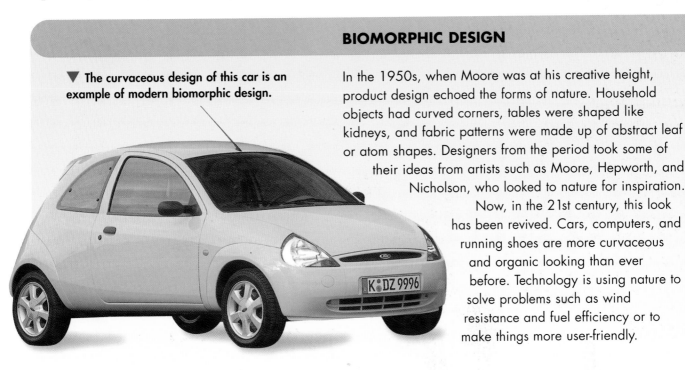

In the 1950s, when Moore was at his creative height, product design echoed the forms of nature. Household objects had curved corners, tables were shaped like kidneys, and fabric patterns were made up of abstract leaf or atom shapes. Designers from the period took some of their ideas from artists such as Moore, Hepworth, and Nicholson, who looked to nature for inspiration. Now, in the 21st century, this look has been revived. Cars, computers, and running shoes are more curvaceous and organic looking than ever before. Technology is using nature to solve problems such as wind resistance and fuel efficiency or to make things more user-friendly.

The Writings of Henry Moore

Moore kept a thorough record of his development as an artist in his notebooks and essays. He had strong opinions on his own work and the work of others, as well as on sculpture in general.

LOOK BEYOND NATURE

One of Moore's main goals was to avoid the tradition of realistic sculpture. Classical statues tried to make stone and marble look like the person it was portraying. Moore thought that stone should look like stone and that nature should not just be copied.

"The first hole in a piece of stone is a revelation. The hole connects one side to the other, making it immediately more three-dimensional."

◀ Moore also understood the importance of "negative space" or the holes around and within a sculpture.

▶ Moore was more concerned about working in a way that was right for the piece than he was about following a specific art style.

"...inspiration will come, as always, from nature and the world around him, from which he learns such principles as balance, rhythm, organic growth of life, attraction and repulsion, harmony and contrast... but mechanical copying of objects and surrounding life will leave him dissatisfied."

▲ Moore makes it clear what he understands the role of an artist to be – to use nature as a springboard but not to imitate it directly.

ART CAN BE ABSTRACT AND SURREAL

There was a lot of debate about which was more important, Abstraction or Surrealism. Moore's work contained elements of both. He sometimes began a drawing of abstract shapes with no particular idea in mind, which is a Surrealist way of working.

"All good art has contained both abstract and surreal elements... order and surprise, intellect and imagination, conscious and unconscious. Both sides of the artist's personality must play their part."

TIMELINE ▶

1898	1918	1922	1928	1937
July 30, 1898 Henry Spencer Moore is born in Castleford, Yorkshire.	**1918** Becomes army physical instructor. Returns to France just as war ends.	**1922** Begins carving in stone and wood. Visits Paris, where he sees Cézanne's work.	**1928** First solo show in London. Meets Herbert Read and Irina Radetsky.	**1937** Visits Picasso's studio in Paris. Produces his first stringed sculpture.
1911 Starts pottery classes with Alice Gostick.	**1919** Returns to Castleford.	**1923** Sells first piece of work as professional artist.	**1929** Marries Irina. They move to Hampstead.	**1938** Starts to use casting rather than direct carving.
1914 World War I begins.	**1920** Wins scholarship to Leeds School of Art. Moore is only sculpture student.	**1924** First exhibition of carvings in London. Starts work as sculpture instructor at Royal College of Art.	**1930** Joins Seven and Five society. Exhibits at Venice Biennale.	**1939** World War II breaks out. Moore resigns from Chelsea College of Art.
1915 Leaves school to become a student teacher.	**1921** Meets Barbara Hepworth. Wins scholarship to London's Royal College of Art. Discovers book *Vision and Design* and the British Museum.	**1925** Departs on travel scholarship to Italy.	**1932** Appointed head of sculpture at Chelsea College of Art.	**1940** Moves to Perry Green.
1916 Works as a teacher.			**1933** Joins Unit One.	**1945** End of World War II.
1917 Joins the army. Is poisoned by mustard gas and returns to England.				**1946** Moore's only child, Mary, is born.

SIZE MATTERS

Moore was very sure about how he wanted a sculpture to appear in the landscape. The size of a piece was very important to him. He also made links between the landscape, the human body, and the material that he worked with.

> *"My own scale? It's just over life size. I think that's because I want my work to stand out-of-doors and be seen in a natural setting, and figures seen out of doors always look slightly smaller than they are."*

▲ Moore didn't want his work to be dwarfed by nature, but to complement it.

> *"Besides the human form, I am tremendously excited by all natural forms, such as cloud formations, birds, trees and their roots, and mountains, which are to me the wrinkling of the earth's surface, like drapery. It is extraordinary how closely ripples in the sand on the seashore resemble the gouge marks in wood carving."*

◀ This quotation by Moore about natural forms helps explain the concept of "truth to material."

HENRY MOORE'S NOTEBOOKS

Moore wrote hundreds of pages of notes and essays about art, as well as producing nearly 1,200 sculptures and at least 5,500 drawings. It helped that he spent time with other artists and intellectuals and was used to talking about his work and ideas.

Throughout his career he kept detailed notebooks charting his thoughts and progress. His notes and drawings of artifacts in the British Museum, for example, provide the most thorough account of primitive art by any modern artist. Although Moore wrote more than most artists, it was only ever to help his artwork.

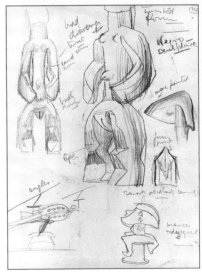

◀ *Studies of Sculpture from the British Museum* page 105, Notebook No.3, 1922-24.

1948	1955	1961	1968	1979
1948 Has solo show at Venice Biennale and wins International Prize for Sculpture.	**1955** Made a Companion of Honour by Queen Elizabeth II. Becomes a Trustee of the National Gallery.	**1961** Elected member of American Academy of Art and Letters.	**1968** Retrospective at the Tate Gallery.	**1979** Develops arthritis and has to work on a smaller scale.
1951 Visits Greece and its classical ruins. Participates in Festival of Britain and has his first retrospective at the Tate Gallery.	**1959** Receives another cascade of awards and has exhibitions worldwide.	**1963** Takes up etching. Receives Order of Merit from Queen Elizabeth II.	**1972** The Henry Moore Trust is set up.	**1982** Henry Moore Centre opens in Leeds. Moore's *Reclining Figure*, 1946, sells for $1,000,000 at an auction in New York.
1953 Wins International Sculpture Prize at second São Paulo Biennale.	**1960** Many German towns commission large bronzes by Moore as public sculptures.	**1964** Appointed member of the Arts Council of Great Britain. Reappointed Trustee of National Gallery.	**1974** The Henry Moore Sculpture Centre is opened in Ontario, Canada.	**1983** Moore's health continues to deteriorate.
		1965 Buys a summer house in Italy. Visits New York.	**1975** Hepworth dies.	**August 31, 1986** Henry Moore dies.
			1977 The Henry Moore Foundation opens. Moore's grandson Gus is born.	

Glossary

Abstraction: an art movement which became influential between 1910 and 1920. Abstract art does not imitate the world around us – it is often impossible to recognize objects, people, or places. Wassily Kandinsky (1866-1944) and Piet Mondrian (1872-1944) were both leading Abstract artists.

artifact: any man-made object of historical importance, such as pottery, jewelery, or textiles.

avant-garde: describes new, experimental, or radical ideas. From the French for vanguard, the first troops in a battle.

Biennale: a prestigious international art exhibition held every two years. Biennales occur in cities around the world, but the most famous one is the Venice Biennale, which first took place in 1895.

Bohemian: describes a person, often an artist or intellectual, who lives in a way that does not follow social conventions.

casting: the process of creating a sculpture by pouring molten metal into a mold.

Classical: describes something from the period of European history which was dominated by the ancient Greek and then Roman civilizations. Classical art usually involved the realistic portrayal of the human figure.

commission: to place an order for something such as a work of art, or a work of art created to order.

critic: a person who makes a living by writing about the arts.

Cubism: an art movement based in Paris from about 1907, led by Georges Braque (1882-1963) and Pablo Picasso (1881-1973). The Cubists painted multiple viewpoints of a person or object so all angles were seen at once.

direct carving: the technique of carving directly into stone or wood using a hammer and chisel.

etching: a print on paper made from an engraved metal plate.

exhibition: a public showing of artworks.

Fascism: an extreme right-wing political system where the government holds total power.

foundry: a place where casting is carried out.

manifesto: a declaration of beliefs.

Modernist: term used to cover all of the art movements of the early 20th century, including Cubism, Surrealism, and Abstraction.

Old Masters: the greatest European painters during the period 1500-1800, including Leonardo da Vinci (1452-1519), Michelangelo (1475-1564), and Rembrandt (1606-69).

primitive art: art created by peoples outside the Western, "developed" world – for example, by Native Americans or by African or Oceanic peoples.

relief: a three-dimensional image projected off a flat surface.

Renaissance: from the French word "rebirth." Describes the European intellectual and artistic movement which began in 14th-century Italy and was at its height (the High Renaissance) in the 16th century. During the Renaissance, Classical ideas were rediscovered, or "reborn."

retrospective: an exhibition showing an artist's development over his or her lifetime.

slag heap: a small hill of waste left by mining.

studio: an artist's workshop.

Surrealism: an intellectual movement that began in the 1920s, which tried to show the life of our unconscious minds and dreams. The Surrealists included artists, writers, and filmmakers.

unconscious: describes the part of a person's mind that lies outside the conscious mind we use in everyday waking life.

Victorian: the period during the reign of Queen Victoria in Great Britain (1837-1901). At this time, British society was morally strict and traditional, and art was based on the classical style.

Museums and Galleries

Works by Moore are exhibited in museums, galleries, streets, squares, towns, and gardens all around the world. Some of the ones listed here are devoted solely to Moore, but most have a wide range of other artists' works on display.

Even if you can't visit any of these galleries yourself, you may be able to visit their web sites. Gallery web sites often show pictures of the artworks they have on display. Some of the web sites even offer virtual tours which allow you to wander around and look at different paintings while sitting comfortably in front of your computer!

Most of the international web sites detailed below include an option that allows you to view them in English.

EUROPE

Didrichsen Art Museum
Kuusilahdenkuja 1
00340 Helsinki
Finland
www.didrichsenmuseum.fi

The Henry Moore Foundation
Dane Tree House
Perry Green
Much Hadham
Hertfordshire, England
SG10 6EE
www.henry-moore-fdn.co.uk

Leeds City Art Gallery
The Headrow
Leeds, England
LS1 3AA
www.leeds.gov.uk/artgallery

Manchester Art Gallery
Mosley Street
Manchester, England
M2 3JL
www.manchestergalleries.org

**The National Museum
and Gallery of Wales**
Cathays Park
Cardiff, Wales
CF10 3NP
www.nmgw.ac.uk/nmgc

Tate Britain
Millbank
London, England
SW1P 4RG
www.tate.org.uk

Ulster Museum
Botanic Gardens
Belfast, Northern Ireland
BT9 5AB
www.ulstermuseum.org.uk

Wakefield Art Gallery
Wentworth Terrace
Wakefield, England
WF1 3QW
www.wakefield.gov.uk

UNITED STATES

Albright-Knox Art Gallery
1285 Elmwood Avenue
Buffalo, NY 14222-1096
www.albrightknox.org

**Hirshhorn Museum and
Sculpture Garden**
Smithsonian Institution
PO Box 37012
Washington, D.C. 20013-7012
www.hirshhorn.si.edu

Metropolitan Museum of Art
1000 Fifth Avenue at 82nd Street
New York, NY 10028-0198
www.metmuseum.org

**The Nelson-Atkins Museum
of Art**
4525 Oak Street
Kansas City, MO 64111-1873
www.nelson-atkins.org/sculpture/
henrymoore/henrymoore.htm

REST OF THE WORLD

Art Gallery of New South Wales
Art Gallery Road, The Domain
Sydney, NSW 2000
Australia
www.artgallery.nsw.gov.au

The Art Gallery of Ontario
317 Dundas Street West
Toronto, Ontario M5T 1G4
Canada
www.ago.net

The Hakone Open Air Museum
1121, Ninotaira, Hakone-machi,
Ashigarashimo-gun, Kanagawa
Japan
www.hakone-oam.or.jp

Index